The Petition to the American Psychological Association

C.A. Childress, Psy.D.

The Childress Institute for Child Development

CONTENTS

The Petition to the American Psychological Association

Seeking Professional Competence in the Assessment, Diagnosis, and Treatment of Attachment-Related Pathology Surrounding Divorce

Prelude:

The lives of children and families are being irrevocably destroyed by the failed response of the mental health system to attachment-related family pathology surrounding divorce.

Children are routinely losing a loving bond to a normal-range and affectionately available parent following divorce, due to the psychologically manipulative and controlling psychopathology of an allied parent who systematically distorts and destroys the child's loving bond to the normal-range parent; and because of the collusive professional incompetence of the mental health system in aiding the enactment of the pathology.

The current response of professional psychology to attachment-related pathology following divorce is to allow the pathological destruction of the child's loving bond to a normal-range and affectionally available parent, and often to collude in enacting the pathology through professional ignorance and sometimes through the active bias born of both ignorance and counter-transference motivations. The current response of professional psychology is rampant with unchecked professional ignorance, incompetence, and the inertia of arrogance that subjects normal-range and loving parents to the most unimaginable trauma possible, the loss of their beloved children.

The professional assessment of attachment-related pathology surrounding divorce is variable, idiosyncratic, and entirely subjective. The diagnosis of attachment related pathology surrounding divorce is often nonexistent or uses subjectively made up diagnostic constructs without established professional definitions. The treatment of attachment-related pathology surrounding divorce is almost universally ineffective in restoring the child's healthy normal-range relationship with the normal-range and affectionally available targeted-rejected parent, and therapy typically lacks any grounding in established forms of psychotherapy. Consistent with the idiosyncratic and entirely subjective diagnostic formulations is often the complete absence of any form or semblance of a treatment plan, with therapists simply making things up as they go, to the great harm and detriment of families.

Children are being routinely and almost universally abandoned to the psychopathology and psychologically abusive parenting of the narcissistic or borderline personality parent who is using the child to meet the emotional and psychological needs of the parent. The lives of children are being destroyed – irrevocably destroyed. The psychological development of children is being destroyed. Childhood occurs only once. Once lost, the times of childhood and their relationships cannot be recovered.

And professional psychology is in collusion with the pathology through profound, rampant, and unchecked professional ignorance and incompetence in the assessment, diagnosis, and treatment of attachment-related family pathology surrounding divorce.

This petition to the American Psychological Association is with the goal of enlisting the support of the APA in affirming its professional code of ethics requiring professional competence from all psychologists, based in the standard and established constructs of professional psychology.

Professional competence is a right granted to all parents for their children and their families, yet it is a right that is currently being denied.

The undersigned are seeking the support of the American Psychological Association in affirming its commitment to the right of all clients who receive psychological services to receive professionally competent practice based in the standard and established constructs and principles of professional psychology, as granted by the Ethical Principles of Psychologists and Code of Conduct of the American Psychological Association.

Whereas;

Article 1: The Pathology

A child rejecting a parent surrounding divorce is fundamentally an attachment-related pathology. The attachment system is the brain system governing all aspects of love and bonding throughout the lifespan, including grief and loss (Ainsworth, 1989; Bowlby, 1969; 1973; 1980; 1988);

From Ainsworth:

"I define an "affectional bond" as a relatively long-enduring tie in which the partner is important as a unique individual and is interchangeable with none other. In an affectional bond, there is a desire to maintain closeness to the partner. In older children and adults, that closeness may to some extent be sustained over time and distance and during absences, but nevertheless there is at least an intermittent desire to reestablish proximity and interaction, and pleasure – often joy – upon reunion. Inexplicable separation tends to cause distress, and permanent loss would cause grief." (Ainsworth, 1989, p. 711)

"An "attachment" is an affectional bond, and hence an attachment figure is never wholly interchangeable with or replaceable by another, even though there may be others to whom one is also attached. In attachments, as in other affectional bonds, there is a need to maintain proximity, distress upon inexplicable separation, pleasure and joy upon reunion, and grief at loss." (Ainsworth, 1989, p. 711)

A child rejecting a relationship with a parent following divorce represents a pathology in the love-and-bonding system of the brain, in the attachment system.

The attachment-related pathology of a child rejecting a normal-range parent surrounding divorce (traditionally called "parental alienation" in the popular culture) is the product of "pathological mourning" (Bowlby, 1980) by an allied narcissistic or borderline personality parent (Kernberg, 1975).

From Bowlby:

"The deactivation of attachment behavior is a key feature of certain common variants of pathological mourning." (Bowlby, 1980, p. 70)

"Disturbances of personality, which include a bias to respond to loss with disordered mourning, are seen as the outcome of one or more deviations in development that can originate or grow worse during any of the years of infancy, childhood and adolescence." (Bowlby, 1980, p. 217)

The narcissistic/(borderline) personality parent in the family is unable to mentalize their experience of sadness (Brüne, Walden, Marc-Andreas, Dimaggio, 2016; Briand-Malenfant, Lecours, & Deschenaux, 2012). As a result, they are unable to process their feelings of sadness surrounding the divorce and instead translate their sadness into anger and aggressive impulses toward the other spouse rather than the actual experience of sadness.

From Kernberg:

"They [narcissists] are especially deficient in genuine feelings of sadness and mournful longing; their incapacity for experiencing depressive reactions is a basic feature of their personalities. When abandoned or disappointed by other people they may show what on the surface looks like depression, but which on further examination emerges as anger and resentment, loaded with revengeful wishes, rather than real sadness for the loss of a person whom they appreciated." (Kernberg, 1975, p. 229)

From Briand-Malenfant, Lecours, and Deschenaux:

> "The results suggest that the experience of suffering (of dysphoria) found in our BPD participants' description of relationship episodes is not yet sadness, being maybe its precursor such as a state of generalized distress or, in other words, an unmentalized form of sadness... This could mean that BPD patients are lacking an access to sadness, creating incapacity to be sad, due to a deficit in mentalization." (Briand-Malenfant, Lecours, & Deschenaux, 2012, p. 952)

The stability of the self-structure organization of the narcissistic personality is vulnerable to rejection by the attachment figure, and the stability of the self-structure organization of the borderline personality is vulnerable to abandonment by the attachment figure. Divorce involves both the rejection and abandonment of the narcissistic/(borderline) spouse and parent by the attachment figure of the other spouse, and divorce exposes to public view the personal inadequacy of the divorced spouse that is leading to their public rejection and abandonment.

From Beck:

> "The core belief of narcissistic personality disorder is one of inferiority or unimportance. This belief is only activated under certain circumstances and thus may be observed mainly in response to conditions of self-esteem threat. Otherwise, the manifest belief is a compensatory attitude of superiority." (Beck et al, 2004, p. 249)

> For the narcissistic personality: "The failure to be superior or regarded as special activates underlying beliefs of inferiority, unimportance, or powerlessness and compensatory strategies of self-protection and self-defense." (Beck et al, 2004, p. 241)

> For the borderline personality: "The specific themes are loneliness, unlovabilty, rejection and abandonment by others, and viewing the self as bad and to be punished." (Beck et al., 2004, p. 192)

Divorce will inherently activate both the rejection and abandonment vulnerabilities of a narcissistic/(borderline) personality parent. The inherent rejection and abandonment by the attachment figure surrounding divorce will threaten to collapse the structure of the narcissistic and borderline personality into an immensely painful inchoate state of disorganization.

In order to stabilize their collapsing personality structure that is being threatened with collapse as a result of the inherent rejection and abandonment surrounding the divorce, the narcissistic/(borderline) personality parent will seek to project their own rejection and abandonment onto the other spouse/(parent) by triangulating the child into the spousal conflict through the formation of a cross-generational coalition with the child against the other parent from which the child is induced into rejecting the other parent (Bowen, 1978; Goldenberg & Goldenberg, 2013; Haley, 1977; Minuchin, 1974; Titelman, 2003), turning the targeted-rejected parent into the rejected parent/(spouse)/(person).

From Haley:

"The people responding to each other in the triangle are not peers, but one of them is of a different generation from the other two... In the process of their interaction together, the person of one generation forms a coalition with the person of the other generation against his peer. By 'coalition' is meant a process of joint action which is *against* the third person... The coalition between the two persons is denied. That is, there is certain behavior which indicates a coalition which, when it is queried, will be denied as a coalition... In essence, the perverse triangle is one in which the separation of generations is breached in a covert way. When this occurs as a repetitive pattern, the system will be pathological. (Haley, 1977, p. 37)

From Minuchin:

"The boundary between the parental subsystem and the child becomes diffuse, and the boundary around the parents-child triad, which should be diffuse, becomes inappropriately rigid. This type of structure is called a rigid triangle... The rigid triangle can also take the form of a stable coalition. One of the parents joins the child in a rigidly bounded cross-generational coalition against the other parent." (Minuchin, 1974, p. 102)

The inability of the narcissistic/(borderline) personality parent to mentalize the experience of sadness surrounding the divorce leads to their pathological mourning in which they translate feelings of sadness and mournful loss into "anger and resentment, loaded with revengeful wishes" toward the attachment figure of the other spouse who is failing to meet the emotional and psychological regulatory needs of the narcissistic/(borderline) spouse.

From Beck:

"Thus, he or she is apt to approach any number of situations feeling automatically entitled to personal gratification. If others fail to satisfy the narcissist's "needs," including the need to look good, or be free from inconvenience, then others "deserve to be punished"... Even when punishing others out of intolerance or entitlement, the narcissist sees this as "a lesson they need, for their own good." (Beck et al., 2004, p. 252).

The narcissistic/(borderline) parent then transfers their own disordered mourning and aberrant mentalization of sadness surrounding the divorce to the child through techniques of psychological manipulation and psychological control of the child within the cross-generational coalition this parent forms with the child.

In his book regarding parental psychological control of children, *Intrusive Parenting: How Psychological Control Affects Children and Adolescents*, published by the American Psychological Association, Brian Barber and his colleague, Elizabeth Harmon, identify over 30 empirically validated scientific studies that have established the construct of parental psychological control of children. Barber and Harmon provide the following definition for the construct of parental psychological control of the child:

"Psychological control refers to parental behaviors that are intrusive and manipulative of children's thoughts, feelings, and attachment to parents. These behaviors appear to be associated with disturbances in the psychoemotional boundaries between the child and parent, and hence with the development of an independent sense of self and identity." (Barber & Harmon, 2002, p. 15)

According to Stone, Bueler, and Barber:

> "The central elements of psychological control are intrusion into the child's psychological world and self-definition and parental attempts to manipulate the child's thoughts and feelings through invoking guilt, shame, and anxiety. Psychological control is distinguished from behavioral control in that the parent attempts to control, through the use of criticism, dominance, and anxiety or guilt induction, the youth's thoughts and feelings rather than the youth's behavior." (Stone, Buehler, & Barber, 2002, p. 57)

Soenens and Vansteenkiste (2010) describe the various methods used to achieve parental psychological control of the child:

> "Psychological control can be expressed through a variety of parental tactics, including (a) guilt-induction, which refers to the use of guilt inducing strategies to pressure children to comply with a parental request; (b) contingent love or love withdrawal, where parents make their attention, interest, care, and love contingent upon the children's attainment of parental standards; (c) instilling anxiety, which refers to the induction of anxiety to make children comply with parental requests; and (d) invalidation of the child's perspective, which pertains to parental constraining of the child's spontaneous expression of thoughts and feelings." (Soenens & Vansteenkiste, 2010, p. 75)

Research by Stone, Buehler, and Barber establishes the link between parental psychological control of children and marital conflict:

> "This study was conducted using two different samples of youth. The first sample consisted of youth living in Knox County, Tennessee. The second sample consisted of youth living in Ogden, Utah." (Stone, Buehler, & Barber, 2002, p. 62)

> "The analyses reveal that variability in psychological control used by parents is not random but it is linked to interparental conflict, particularly covert conflict. Higher levels of covert conflict in the marital relationship heighten the likelihood that parents would use psychological control with their children." (Stone, Buehler, & Barber, 2002, p. 86)

Stone, Buehler, and Barber provide an explanation for their finding that intrusive parental psychological control of children is related to high inter-spousal conflict:

> "The concept of triangles "describes the way any three people relate to each other and involve others in emotional issues between them" (Bowen, 1989, p. 306). In the anxiety-filled environment of conflict, a third person is triangulated, either temporarily or permanently, to ease the anxious feelings of the conflicting partners. By default, that third person is exposed to an anxiety-provoking and disturbing atmosphere. For example, a child might become the scapegoat or focus of attention, thereby transferring the tension from the marital dyad to the parent-child dyad. Unresolved tension in the marital relationship might spill over to the parent-child relationship through parents' use of psychological control as a way of securing and maintaining a strong emotional alliance and level of support from the child. As a consequence, the triangulated youth might feel pressured or obliged to listen to or agree with one parent's complaints against the other. The resulting enmeshment and cross-generational coalition would exemplify parents' use of psychological control to coerce and maintain a parent-youth

emotional alliance against the other parent (Haley, 1976; Minuchin, 1974)." (Stone, Buehler, & Barber, 2002, p. 86-87)

The psychological control of the child occurs in a pathological parent-child context of an "invalidating environment," described by Linehan and Koerner, that interferes with the child's mentalization of self-experience.

From Linehan and Koerner:

> "A defining characteristic of the invalidating environment is the tendency of the family to respond erratically or inappropriately to private experience and, in particular, to be insensitive (i.e., nonresponsive) to private experience… Invalidating environments contribute to emotional dysregulation by: (1) failing to teach the child to label and modulate arousal, (2) failing to teach the child to tolerate stress, (3) failing to teach the child to trust his or her own emotional responses as valid interpretations of events, and (4) actively teaching the child to invalidate his or her own experiences by making it necessary for the child to scan the environment for cues about how to act and feel." (Linehan & Koerner, 1993, p. 111-112)

The narcissistic/(borderline) personality parent's inability to mentalize and thereby psychologically process the experience of sadness created by the divorce results in their "pathological mourning" of the divorce that is then transferred to the child's experience through manipulative techniques of psychologically controlling the child within a relational environment that invalidates the child's authenticity to create a cross-generational coalition of the narcissistic/(borderline) parent with the child against the targeted parent, in which the child is manipulated and induced to terminate the child's relationship with the targeted parent.

A structural family diagram of this cross-generational coalition and the cutoff in the child's relationship with a parent created by the cross-generational coalition is provided on page 42 of Salvador Minuchin's book *Family Healing* (1993) with co-author Michael Nichols.

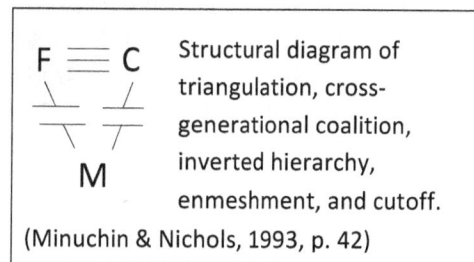

Structural diagram of triangulation, cross-generational coalition, inverted hierarchy, enmeshment, and cutoff.
(Minuchin & Nichols, 1993, p. 42)

As noted by Bowlby in his description of pathological mourning, the disordered mourning is created in the distorted childhood experiences of the parent that created this parent's personality pathology. The current attachment-related pathology, expressed as the child's rejection of a normal-range parent following divorce, represents the trans-generational transmission of attachment trauma from the childhood of the allied narcissistic/(borderline) parent to the current family relationships, mediated by the personality disorder pathology of the parent that is itself a product of this parent's childhood attachment trauma.

The childhood attachment trauma of the narcissistic/(borderline) parent that is creating this parent's incapacity to mentalize and process sadness, leading to this parent's pathological mourning surrounding the divorce, is contained in internalized schemas of attachment expectations (called "internal working models" of attachment by Bowlby, 1969; 1973; 1980).

From Beck:

"Evaluation of the particular demands of a situation precedes and triggers an adaptive (or maladaptive) strategy. How a situation is evaluated depends in part, at least, on the relevant underlying beliefs. These beliefs are embedded in more or less stable structures, labeled "schemas," that select and synthesize incoming data." (Beck et al., 2004, p. 17)

"The content of the schemas may deal with personal relationships, such as attitudes toward the self or others, or impersonal categories... When schemas are latent, they are not participating in information processing; when activated they channel cognitive processing from the earliest to the final stages... When hypervalent, these idiosyncratic schemas displace and probably inhibit other schemas that may be more adaptive or more appropriate for a given situation. They consequently introduce a systematic bias into information processing." (Beck et al., 2004, p. 27)

"In personality disorders, the schemas are part of normal, everyday processing of information." (Beck et al., 2004, p. 27)

"When particular schemas are hypervalent, the threshold for activation of the constituent schemas is low: they are readily triggered by a remote or trivial stimulus. They are also "prepotent"; that is, they readily supersede more appropriate schemas or configurations in processing information." (Beck et al., 2004, p. 28)

From Bowlby:

"No variables, it is held, have more far-reaching effects on personality development than have a child's experiences within his family: for, starting during the first months of his relations with his mother figure, and extending through the years of childhood and adolescence in his relations with both parents, he builds up working models of how attachment figures are likely to behave towards him in any of a variety of situations; and on those models are based all his expectations, and therefore all his plans for the rest of his life." (Bowlby, 1973, p. 369).

The childhood attachment trauma that creates the damaged self-structure of pathological narcissism and borderline personality pathology can emerge from a variety of childhood attachment trauma experiences, but increasing research is focusing on the role of disorganized attachment created by a parent who is simultaneously a source of threat and a source of nurture.

From Beck:

"Various studies have found that patients with BPD are characterized by disorganized attachment representations (Fonagy et al., 1996; Patrick et al, 1994). Such attachment representations appear to be typical for persons with unresolved childhood traumas, especially when parental figures were involved, with direct, frightening behavior by the parent. Disorganized attachment is considered to result from an unresolvable situation for the child when "the parent is at the same time the source of fright as well as the potential haven of safety" (van IJzendoorn, Schuengel, & Bakermans-Kranburg, 1999, p. 226)." (Beck et al., 2004, p. 191)

"Some traumatic experiences may have taken place at a very early age, notably the kind of punishing, abandoning, rejecting responses of the caretaker that led to disorganized attachment." (Beck et al., 2004, p. 191)

"Arntz (1994) hypothesized that childhood traumas underlie the formation of core schemas, which in their turn, lead to the development of BPD." (Beck et al., 2004, p 192)

From Stepp, et al.:

"Individuals with BPD tend to have attachment styles classified as disorganized and unresolved (Levy, 2005)" (Stepp, et al., 2011, p. 3)

Levy, K.N. (2005). The implications of attachment theory and research for understanding borderline personality disorder. Development and Psychopathology, 17, p. 959-986

From Trippany, Helm, and Simpson:

"Research shows that disturbances with attachment and bonding in early childhood affect personality development and healthy interpersonal functioning as an adult, often resulting in the development of personality disorders such as BPS." (Trippany, Helm, and Simpson, p. 100)

Increasing research is also linking the formation of borderline personality characteristics to sexual abuse victimization during childhood (Ogata, et al., 1990; Sieswerda, Arntz, Mertens, & Vertommen, 2006; Trippany, Helm, & Simpson, 2006; Bailey & Shriver, 1999)

Childhood attachment trauma becomes instantiated into the neural networks of the attachment system as schemas (internal working models) of attachment expectations, that then guide future responding to attachment-related challenges that reactivate these internalized trauma networks.

From van der Kolk:

"When the trauma fails to be integrated into the totality of a person's life experiences, the victim remains fixated on the trauma. Despite avoidance of emotional involvement, traumatic memories cannot be avoided: even when pushed out of waking consciousness, they come back in the form of reenactments, nightmares, or feelings related to the trauma... Recurrences may continue throughout life during periods of stress." (van der Kolk, 1987, p. 5)

"Victims of trauma respond to contemporary stimuli as if the trauma had returned, without conscious awareness that past injury rather than current stress is the basis of their physiologic emergency responses. The hyperarousal interferes with their ability to make calm and rational assessments and prevents resolution and integration of the trauma... People who have been exposed to highly stressful stimuli develop long-term potentiation of memory tracts that are reactivated at times of subsequent arousal. This activation explains how current stress is experienced as a return of the trauma; it causes a return to earlier behavior patterns." (van der Kolk, 1989, p. 226)

From Beck:

"The conceptualization of the core pathology of BPD as stemming from a highly frightened, abused child who is left alone in a malevolent world, longing for safety and help but distrustful because of fear of further abuse and abandonment, is highly related to the model developed by Young (McGinn & Young, 1996)... Young elaborated on an idea, in the 1980s introduced by Aaron Beck in clinical workshops (D.M. Clark, personal communication), that some pathological states of patients with BPD are a sort of regression into intense emotional states experienced as a child. Young conceptualized such states as schema modes." (Beck et al., 2004, p. 199)

"Young hypothesized that four schema modes are central to BPD: the abandoned child mode (the present author suggests to label it the abused and abandoned child); the angry/impulsive child mode; the punitive parent mode, and the detached protector mode… The abused and abandoned child mode denotes the desperate state the patient may be in related to (threatened) abandonment and abuse the patient has experienced as a child. Typical core beliefs are that other people are malevolent, cannot be trusted, and will abandon or punish you, especially when you become intimate with them." (Beck et al., 2004, p. 199)

From Trippany, Helm, and Simpson:

"Victims of past trauma may respond to contemporary events as though the trauma has returned and re-experience the hyperarousal that accompanied the initial trauma." (Trippany, Helm, and Simpson, p. 100)

Pearlman and Courtois identify the pattern of the attachment trauma reenactment narrative:

"Reenactments of the traumatic past are common in the treatment of this population and frequently represent either explicit or coded repetitions of the unprocessed trauma in an attempt at mastery. Reenactments can be expressed psychologically, relationally, and somatically and may occur with conscious intent or with little awareness." (Pearlman & Courtois, 2005, p. 455)

"One primary transference-countertransference dynamic involves reenactment of familiar roles of victim-perpetrator-rescuer-bystander in the therapy relationship. Therapist and client play out these roles, often in complementary fashion with one another, as they relive various aspects of the client's early attachment relationships." (Pearlman & Courtois, 2005, p. 455)

Sigmund Freud also identified the repetition of trauma. According to Prager:

"Freud suggests that overwhelming experience is taken up into what passes as normal ego and as permanent trends within it; and, in this manner, passes trauma from one generation to the next. In this way, trauma expresses itself as time standing still… Traumatic guilt --- for a time buried except through the character formation of one generation after the next --- finds expression in an unconscious reenactment of the past in the present." (Prager, 2003, p. 176)

From Freud:

"Here we may note two important points. The effects of the trauma are twofold, positive and negative. The former are endeavors to revive the trauma, to remember the forgotten experience, or, better still, to make it real – to live it once more through a repetition of it; if it was an early affective relationship it is revived in an analogous connection to another person. These endeavours are summed up in the terms "fixation to the trauma" and "repetition-compulsion." (Freud, 1939, p. 122)

The attachment trauma pattern of the "abusive parent"/"victimized child"/"protective parent" that is embedded in the schema patterns of the narcissistic/(borderline) parent's internal working models of attachment is reactivated by the rejection and abandonment of the spousal attachment figure in the divorce, creating the psychological context for transferring the trauma reenactment narrative from the childhood attachment trauma of the narcissistic/(borderline) parent to the current family relationships.

The key to creating this false trauma reenactment narrative in the current family relationships is to convince the child to adopt the role as a supposedly "victimized child" in the false trauma reenactment narrative of the narcissistic/(borderline) parent. This is accomplished through manipulative parental communications and psychologically controlling parenting practices that incorporate a distorted parental mentalization of the child's sadness surrounding the divorce as instead representing "anger and resentment, loaded with revengeful wishes" directed toward the other parent.

Once the child adopts the false role in the trauma reenactment narrative as the supposedly "victimized child" of the normal-range parenting of the targeted parent, this "victimized child" role automatically imposes the "abusive parent" role in the trauma reenactment narrative onto the targeted parent, irrespective of the actual parenting of the targeted parent, and the "victimized child" role simultaneously allows the narcissistic/(borderline parent) to adopt and then conspicuously display the coveted role as the all-wonderful "protective parent" in the false trauma reenactment narrative created from this parent's childhood attachment trauma.

According to Prager:

> "Trauma, as a wound that never heals, succeeds in transforming the subsequent world into its own image, secure in its capacity to re-create the experience for time immemorial. It succeeds in passing the experience from one generation to the next. The present is lived *as if* it were the past. The result is that the next generation is deprived of its sense of social location and its capacity to creatively define itself autonomously from the former… when time becomes distorted as a result of overwhelming events, the natural distance between generations, demarcated by the passing of time and changing experience, becomes obscured." (Prager, 2003, p. 176)

The attachment system is the brain system that governs all aspects of love and bonding throughout the lifespan, including grief and loss. Divorce activates the schema patterns embedded in the brain's attachment networks (the internal working models of attachment) to mediate the emotional and psychological loss of the spousal attachment figure.

The divorce activates two separate sets of representational networks in the attachment networks of the narcissistic/(borderline) parent, one embedded in the trauma schema patterns of the internal working models of childhood attachment trauma, and the second set representing the current family members, the targeted parent, the current child, and the self-representation of the narcissistic/(borderline) parent.

The concurrent co-activation of two sets of representational networks in the attachment system of the narcissistic/(borderline) parent creates a psychological fusion – a psychological equivalency – of these two representational networks. In the mind of the narcissistic/(borderline) parent, the targeted parent becomes the supposedly "abusive parent" from the childhood trauma experience of the narcissistic/(borderline) parent, while the current child becomes psychologically equivalent to the "victimized child" from the narcissistic/(borderline) parent's own childhood trauma experience, and the narcissistic/(borderline) parent then adopts and conspicuously displays the coveted role as the all-wonderful "protective parent."

In addition, the splitting pathology of the narcissistic/(borderline) parent cannot accommodate to ambivalence. When the polarization of the splitting pathology inherent to the narcissistic/(borderline) personality is added to the cross-generational coalition with the child, a particularly malignant and virulent form of cross-generational coalition is created in which the child seeks to entirely terminate the child's relationship with the normal-range and affectionally available parent.

The pathology of splitting cannot accommodate to ambivalence. In the mind of the narcissistic/(borderline) parent, when the current spouse becomes an ex-spouse they must also become an ex-parent as well in order to maintain the consistency required by the splitting pathology; the ex-wife must become an ex-mother, and the ex-husband must become an ex-father. This is a neurologically imposed imperative of the splitting pathology inherent to the narcissistic and borderline personality dynamics.

The attachment-related pathology commonly referred to as "parental alienation" in the popular culture involves a complex blend of four different but interrelated pathologies:

- **Attachment-Related Pathology:** Pathological mourning creating the child's rejection of a normal-range and affectionally available parent;

- **Personality Disorder Pathology:** Parental narcissistic and borderline personality pathology in which the child's induced rejection of the other parent is being created and used to stabilize the collapsing personality structure of the narcissistic/borderline pathology in response to the rejection and abandonment inherent to divorce and the public exposure through the divorce rejection of the personal inadequacy of the narcissistic/(borderline) spouse (public humiliation);

- **Family Systems Pathology:** The triangulation of the child into the inter-spousal conflict through the formation of a cross-generational coalition of the child with the allied narcissistic/(borderline) parent against the other parent and the subsequent emotional cutoff created in the parent-child relationship;

- **Complex Trauma Pathology:** The trans-generational transmission of attachment trauma from the childhood of the narcissistic/(borderline) parent to the current family relationships through the false trauma reenactment pattern of "abusive parent"/"victimized child"/"protective parent" that is embedded in the schema patterns (internal working models) of the narcissistic/(borderline) parent's attachment networks.

Professional competence in the assessment, diagnosis, and treatment of attachment-related pathology surrounding divorce requires professional-level knowledge and expertise in all four of these domains of knowledge.

Article 2: The Attachment System

The attachment system is the brain system governing all aspects of love and bonding throughout the lifespan, including grief and loss. A child's rejection of a relationship with a parent represents an attachment-related pathology. The characteristic functioning of the attachment system has been extensively researched and documented in the scientific literature.

The attachment system functions in characteristic ways, and it dysfunctions in characteristic ways. In response to problematic parenting, the attachment system responds by MORE strongly motivating the child to bond to the problematic parent. This is called an "insecure attachment" (Bretherton, 1992). There are various patterns displayed by insecure attachment, but they all seek to maximize the child's attachment bond to the problematic parent, depending on the nature of the problematic parenting the child is exposed to.

The attachment system is a "goal-corrected" motivational system, meaning that it ALWAYS maintains the goal of forming an attachment bond to the parent. In response to problematic parenting, the attachment system changes HOW it tries to achieve this attachment bond, but it always tries to form an attached bond to the parent. This is because the child's attachment bond to the parent provides a significant survival advantage to the child.

The attachment system evolved through the selective targeting of children by predators. Children who formed strong attachment bonds to parents received parental protection from predators so that their genes for forming strong attachment bonds to parents increased in the collective gene pool.

Children who formed weaker attachment bonds to parents became more likely to fall prey to predators (and other environmental dangers) at higher rates, so their genes for forming weaker attachment bonds were systematically eliminated from the collective gene pool. Over the millennia of systematic evolutionary pressures applied by the selective predation of children, a very powerful and highly resilient primary motivational system developed in the brain that strongly motivates children to form strong attachment bonds to parents; even to bad parents, and especially to bad parents.

From Bowlby:

> "The biological function of this behavior is postulated to be protection, especially protection from predators." (Bowlby, 1980, p. 3)

Problematic parenting creates a parent-child relationship called an "insecure attachment." An insecure attachment more strongly motivates children to form an attachment bond to the problematic parent. This is because bad parenting more fully exposes children to predation and other environmental dangers. Children who rejected bad parents were more likely to die from predation and other environmental dangers, thereby removing the genes for rejecting bad parents from the collective gene pool. On the other hand, children who became more strongly motivated to form an attachment bond to a bad parent became more likely to receive parental protection, so their genes for more strongly motivating the child to form an attachment bond to a bad parent increased in the collective gene pool.

This increased child motivation to bond to an abusive parent was demonstrated in the classic bonding experiments involving maternal deprivation in monkeys conducted by Harlow.

From Seay, Alexander, and Harlow:

> "All seven of these MM monkeys [motherless monkeys] were totally inadequate mothers... Initially, the MM monkeys tended to ignore or withdraw from their babies even when the infants were disengaged and screaming... Later the motherless monkeys ignored, rejected, and were physically abusive to their infants... A surprising phenomena was the universally persisting attempts by the infants to attach to the mother's body regardless of neglect or physical punishment. When the infants failed to attach to the ventral surface of the mother, they would cling to the dorsal surface and attempt to move to the mother's ventral surface." (Seay, Alexander, and Harlow, 1964, p. 353)

From van der Kolk:

> "Increased imprinting to abusing objects has been demonstrated in birds (33), dogs (34), monkeys (35, 36), and human beings (7). Sackett et al. (37) found that monkeys raised by abusive mothers cling to them more than average: The immediate consequence of maternal rejection is the accentuation of proximity seeking on the part of the infant. After similar experiments, Harlow and Harlow (35) concluded: "Instead of producing experimental neurosis we had achieved a technique for enhancing maternal attachment." (van der Kolk, 1987, p. 34)

From Raineki, Moriceau, and Sullivan:

> "A potential evolutionary explanation suggests selection pressures supported infants that remained attached because it increased the probability of survival. From an adaptive point of view, perhaps it is better for an altricial animal to remain attached to an abusive caregiver than receive no care." (Raineki, Moriceau, & Sullivan, p. 1143)

The extensive research on the characteristic patterns of functioning and dysfunctioning of the attachment system all indicates that problematic parenting creates an *insecure attachment* that <u>increases</u> the child's motivation to bond to the problematic parent.

> "The paradoxical finding that the more punishment a juvenile receives the stronger becomes its attachment to the punishing figure, very difficult to explain in any other theory, is compatible with the view that the function of attachment behavior is protection from predators." (Bowlby, 1969, p. 227)

In psychologically assessing attachment bonding, a ***secure*** and healthy parent-child attachment bond is evidenced by the child's relaxed willingness to separate from the parent because the child is *secure* in the parent's love and protection. An ***insecure*** parent-child attachment relationship, on the other hand, is evidenced by a hyper-bonding display between the parent and child in which the child's focus is directed toward the parent (i.e., the child is *insecure* in the emotional availability of the parent and so the child must constantly strive to recognize and meet the emotional and psychological needs of the parent).

From Kerig:

> "In order to carve out an island of safety and responsivity in an unpredictable, harsh, and depriving parent-child relationship, children of highly maladaptive parents may become precocious caretakers who are adept at reading the cues and meeting the needs of those

around them. The ensuing preoccupied attachment with the parent interferes with the child's development of important ego functions, such as self organization, affect regulation, and emotional object constancy." (Kerig, 2005, p. 14)

The child's attachment bonding motivations toward a parent can, however, be artificially suppressed. Since the attachment system is a predator-driven system it is highly sensitive to parental signals of anxiety and parental threat perception. From the perspective of the attachment system, even subtle displays of parental anxiety and anxious concern for the child's safety will trigger the child's predator-driven motivation to remain in the protective proximity of the anxious and over-concerned parent who is signaling that there is a threat to the child.

If one parent signals to the child through this parent's anxious concern that a relationship with the other parent represents a threat to the child, then this will trigger the child's attachment system to terminate exploratory behavior away from the anxious-concerned parent and simultaneously motivate the child to remain in the "protective" proximity of the supposedly "protective" parent (i.e., the parent who is signaling anxiety). The supposedly "protective" parent's emotional signals of anxiety will essentially act to define the other parent as representing a "predator threat" relative to the child's attachment bonding motivations toward this parent.

Defining the other parent as representing a "predator threat" to the child will artificially suppress the child's attachment bonding motivations toward the other parent. However, if the child is allowed to separate sufficiently from the anxiety signals of the supposedly "protective parent," then the normal-range functioning of the child's attachment system toward the other parent will resume and will once again motivate the child to form an affectionally attached bond to this parent.

Attachment-related pathology is always the product of pathogenic parenting (patho=pathology; genic=genesis, creation). Pathogenic parenting refers to the creation of psychopathology in the child through aberrant and distorted parenting practices. The construct of pathogenic parenting is an established construct in both developmental and clinical psychology and is most often used in reference to attachment-related pathology since the attachment system <u>never</u> spontaneously dysfunctions, but ONLY becomes dysfunctional in response to pathogenic parenting.

The diagnostic issue in assessing pathogenic parenting is to determine which parent is creating the child's attachment-related pathology; is it the targeted-rejected parent through abusive parenting practices (such as physical or sexual abuse of the child), or is it the allied and supposedly "favored" parent through the formation of a cross-generational coalition with the child against the other parent?

Article 3: Professional Competence & Harm to the Client

Standard 2.01a of the APA ethics code requires professional competence:

2.01 Boundaries of Competence
(a) Psychologists provide services, teach, and conduct research with populations and in areas only within the boundaries of their competence, based on their education, training, supervised experience, consultation, study, or professional experience.

Standard 2.03 of the APA ethics code requires that psychologists take ongoing steps to maintain their professional competence:

2.03 Maintaining Competence
Psychologists undertake ongoing efforts to develop and maintain their competence.

Standard 9.01a of the APA ethics code requires that psychologists base their diagnostic statements and forensic testimony on assessments sufficient to substantiate their findings:

9.01 Bases for Assessments
(a) Psychologists base the opinions contained in their recommendations, reports, and diagnostic or evaluative statements, including forensic testimony, on information and techniques sufficient to substantiate their findings.

Standard 3.04 of the APA ethics code requires that psychologists take reasonable steps to avoid harm to their clients:

3.04 Avoiding Harm
(a) Psychologists take reasonable steps to avoid harming their clients/patients, students, supervisees, research participants, organizational clients, and others with whom they work, and to minimize harm where it is foreseeable and unavoidable.

The appropriate assessment, accurate diagnosis, and effective treatment of attachment-related pathology surrounding divorce requires professional-level expertise in four domains of professional knowledge:

- **The Attachment System:** Mental health professionals who are assessing, diagnosing, and treating attachment-related pathology need to be professionally knowledgeable and competent in the attachment system, what it is, how it functions, and how it characteristically dysfunctions.

  Failure to possess professional-level knowledge regarding the attachment system when assessing, diagnosing, and treating attachment-related pathology would represent practice beyond the boundaries of professional competence in **violation of Standard 2.01a of the APA ethics code**.

- **Personality Disorder Pathology:** Mental health professionals who are assessing, diagnosing, and treating personality disorder related pathology as it is affecting family relationships need to be professionally knowledgeable and competent in personality disorder pathology, what it is, how it functions, and how it characteristically affects family relationships following divorce.

Failure to possess professional-level knowledge regarding personality disorder pathology when assessing, diagnosing, and treating personality disorder related pathology in the family would represent practice beyond the boundaries of professional competence in **violation of Standard 2.01a of the APA ethics code**.

- **Family Systems Pathology:** Mental health professionals who are assessing, diagnosing, and treating families need to be professionally knowledgeable and competent in the functioning of family systems and the principles of family systems therapy.

   Failure to possess professional-level knowledge regarding the functioning of family systems and the principles of family systems therapy when assessing, diagnosing, and treating family pathology would represent practice beyond the boundaries of professional competence in **violation of Standard 2.01a of the APA ethics code**.

- **Complex Trauma Pathology:** Mental health professionals who are assessing, diagnosing, and treating the trans-generational transmission of complex trauma need to be professionally knowledgeable and competent in the nature of complex trauma, as expressed both individually and through family relationships.

   Failure to possess professional-level knowledge regarding the trans-generational transmission and expression of complex trauma when assessing, diagnosing, and treating family pathology involving complex trauma would represent practice beyond the boundaries of professional competence in **violation of Standard 2.01a of the APA ethics code**.

Failure by psychologists to take active ongoing steps to maintain their professional competence would represent a **violation of Standard 2.03 of the APA ethics code** regarding maintaining professional competence. This would include a psychologist's rejection of client-initiated efforts to appropriately provide educational materials to the psychologist regarding the required domains of professional knowledge needed for professional competence in the assessment, diagnosis, and treatment of attachment related pathology surrounding divorce.

The attachment system never spontaneously dysfunctions. Attachment-related pathology is always the product of pathogenic parenting. If the assessing psychologist has not even assessed for pathogenic parenting surrounding attachment-related pathology then the diagnostic statements and forensic testimony of the psychologist cannot possibly be based on "information and techniques sufficient to substantiate their findings," and would therefore represent a **violation of Standard 9.01a of the APA ethics code**. All assessments of attachment-related pathology surrounding divorce must contain the assessment (and documentation of the assessment findings) of possible pathogenic parenting by the targeted-rejected parent (child abuse), and of possible pathogenic parenting by the allied and supposedly "favored parent" (a cross-generational coalition with the child against the other parent).

In all cases of attachment-related pathology surrounding divorce, failure to conduct and document an appropriate professional assessment for pathogenic parenting that is creating the attachment-related pathology would represent a **violation of Standard 9.01a of the APA ethics code**.

If a failure to establish professional competence and then maintain professional competence, and to conduct an appropriate assessment "sufficient to substantiate" the psychologist's diagnosis and forensic testimony, leads to harm inflicted to the client, then the psychologist's failure to establish professional competence, to maintain professional competence, and to conduct an appropriate assessment would represent a **violation of Standard 3.04 of the APA ethics code** requiring psychologists to avoid harming their clients.

Statements of Concern:

1. Psychologists are currently assessing, diagnosing, and treating attachment-related pathology surrounding divorce without the required professional-level knowledge regarding the attachment system, personality disorder pathology, family systems constructs, and complex trauma pathology necessary for professional competence, in violation of Standards 2.01a and 2.03 of the APA ethics code.

2. As a result, their assessments of attachment-related pathology surrounding divorce are inadequate and are not based on information sufficient to substantiate their diagnostic statements and forensic testimony, in violation of Standard 9.01a of the APA ethics code.

3. Their failure to possess adequate professional knowledge required for professionally competent assessment, diagnosis, and treatment of attachment-related pathology surrounding divorce, yet their continued assessment, diagnosis, and treatment efforts with attachment-related pathology surrounding divorce is resulting in severe and irrevocable harm to children and families, in violation of Standard 3.04 of the APA ethics code.

4. In the absence of active support from the American Psychological Association that affirms the requirements set forth in the APA ethics code that all psychologists fully abide by Standards 2.01a, 2.03, 9.01a, and 3.04 of the APA ethics code, the only recourse left to targeted parents and their children to achieve professional competence in the assessment, diagnosis, and treatment of their children and families is through licensing board complaints and malpractice lawsuits against each individual psychologist, forcing them to demonstrate their "education, training, supervised experience, consultation, study, or professional experience" in all four domains of professional knowledge required for professional competence; the attachment system, personality disorder pathology, family systems therapy, and complex trauma pathology.

Article 4: Remedies Sought from the APA

Parents and children who are experiencing the deeply damaging consequences of rampant and unchecked professional ignorance and incompetence surrounding the assessment, diagnosis, and treatment of the attachment-related pathology following divorce being evidenced in their families are seeking the following remedies from the American Psychological Association to the severe emotional and psychological suffering caused by the rampant and unchecked professional ignorance and incompetence in professional psychology:

1. Immediate Press Release Statement

Targeted parents and their children are seeking an immediate press release statement from the American Psychological Association affirming its commitment to Standards 2.01a, 2.03, 9.01a, and 3.04 of the APA ethics code and asserting the requirement that all psychologists maintain the highest standards of professional practice relative to these Standards.

Targeted parents and their children request the APA press release be in the following format:

"The professional assessment, diagnosis, and treatment of attachment-related pathology surrounding divorce can include a complex array of factors that requires a high level of professional expertise in the relevant domains of professional pathology, potentially including a professional-level understanding regarding the attachment system, the possible role of parental personality pathology in distorting family relationships following divorce, relevant constructs from family systems therapy, and the potential impact of complex trauma manifesting within the current family relationships and also transmitted across generations. The American Psychological Association wishes to reaffirm its commitment that all psychologists are expected to maintain the highest standards of professional practice relative to meeting the requirements of Standards 2.01a, 2.03, 9.01a, and 3.04 of the APA ethics code regarding professional competence and the duty of care for clients."

2. Change to the APA Statement on Parental Alienation Syndrome

The construct of "parental alienation" and its associated syndrome proposal of "Parental Alienation Syndrome" (PAS) is a deeply flawed professional construct. In proposing a new form of pathology called "Parental Alienation Syndrome," Richard Gardner led professional psychology away from the use of standard and established constructs and principles and into the wilderness of supposedly new forms of pathology which are alleged to be unique in all of mental health. By leaving the path of established professional constructs and principles, the construct of "parental alienation" (and it's associated PAS syndrome construct) has created the current circumstances allowing for, indeed inviting, the rampant and unchecked professional ignorance and incompetence regarding pathology that is, in truth, created by defined and fully established constructs from established domains of professional knowledge (i.e., the attachment system, personality disorder pathology, family systems therapy, and complex trauma).

Gardner was correct in identifying the existence of an attachment-related pathology surrounding divorce. However, he was incorrect in identifying it as a supposedly new form of pathology unique in all of mental health that required a new and unique set of symptom identifiers that he simply made up for this supposedly new form of pathology.

It is long past overdue for professional psychology to return to standard and established professional constructs and principles to define and identify pathology. John Bowlby, Salvador Minuchin, Aaron Beck, Theodore Millon, Bessel van der Kolk, Jay Haley, Murray Bowen, Otto Kernberg, Mary Ainsworth, Peter Fonagy, Daniel Stern, Heinz Kohut, Marsha Linehan, Edward Tronick, Alan Sroufe are among the preeminent luminaries in professional psychology. Attachment-related family pathology surrounding divorce is fully capable of being defined, diagnosed, and treated using the standard and established constructs and principles of professional psychology.

As professional psychology leaves the wilderness of "new forms of pathology" proposals represented by the constructs of "parental alienation" and "Parental Alienation Syndrome," it will be important that the American Psychological Association adopts a balanced and accurate position regarding the nature of attachment-related pathology surrounding divorce. The construct of Parental Alienation Syndrome is not a well-conceived or executed professional definition of pathology. However, this does not mean that a coherent attachment-related pathology does not exist surrounding divorce, as defined within the standard and established constructs and principles of professional psychology.

Children and families experiencing severe attachment-related pathology following divorce that is created through the trans-generational transmission of attachment trauma from the childhood of a narcissistic/(borderline) parent to the current family relationships, mediated by the personality disorder pathology of this parent who has formed a cross-generational coalition with the child against the other parent, merits full professional acknowledgement and recognition of the pathology. For the purposes of acknowledging the existence of the pathology, a convenient label for the complex attachment-related family systems personality disorder complex trauma pathology is needed. For the purposes of this petition statement, the label used will be the Bowlby-Minuchin-Beck model of attachment-based "parental alienation" (AB-PA).

This label's identification of three of the leading figures in professional psychology indicates that the pathology is being defined through the standard and established constructs and principles of professional psychology. The designation of this label as an attachment-based model of the pathology highlights that a child rejecting a parent is foundationally an attachment-related pathology. The use of the term "parental alienation" links this label to the popular culture label for the pathology, but by placing the term in quotes this label indicates that the construct of "parental alienation" is not a defined construct in professional psychology (except as defined through the Bowlby-Minuchin-Beck model of attachment-based "parental alienation").

The complex nature of the pathology also requires a high-level of professional knowledge and expertise for professionally competent assessment, diagnosis, and treatment using the standard and established constructs and principles of professional psychology. The degree of professional knowledge required for professional competence with this complex type of attachment-related family pathology warrants the designation of children and families who are experiencing attachment-related pathology surrounding divorce as representing a special population who require specialized professional knowledge and expertise for the competent assessment, diagnosis, and treatment of this pathology.

The remedy sought from the American Psychological Association seeks a change in the official APA position *Statement on Parental Alienation Syndrome* to reflect a balanced and professionally responsible position that addresses the following two concerns:

A. **Acknowledgement of the Pathology**: The APA position statement should formally acknowledge that attachment-related family pathology surrounding divorce exists, using whatever label for the pathology the APA wishes. The label can be attachment-related pathology, the trans-generational transmission of attachment trauma pathology, the Bowlby-Minuchin-Beck model of attachment-related pathology surrounding divorce, or any other label. The APA simply needs to acknowledge that the pathology exists.

B. **Special Population Status:** The APA position statement should formally designate children and families experiencing attachment-related pathology surrounding divorce as a special population requiring specialized professional knowledge and expertise to competently assess, diagnose, and treat.

The recommended format for this statement would be:

Statement on Attachment-Related Family Pathology Surrounding Divorce

"Attachment-related family pathology can sometimes emerge in families surrounding divorce. The complexity of attachment-related family pathology surrounding divorce can involve a complex interplay of individual and family systems factors that requires specialized professional knowledge and expertise to competently assess, accurately diagnose, and effectively treat. Because of its inherent complexity, children and families who are experiencing attachment-related family pathology following divorce warrant the designation as a "special population" who require specialized professional knowledge and expertise in a variety of professional domains of knowledge needed for competent assessment, accurate diagnosis, and effective treatment. The American Psychological Association encourages all mental health professionals to achieve the highest level of professional knowledge and expertise required to serve the best interests of their clients."

3. Conference of Experts

The American Psychological Association should convene a high-level conference of experts to produce a white paper regarding the issues surrounding attachment-related pathology following divorce. This high-level conference should invite two representatives from each of the following domains:

- Attachment pathology expertise
- Personality disorder pathology expertise
- Family systems therapy expertise
- Complex trauma expertise
- Client-parent representation

One member of each pair of representatives should be designated as a presenter, the other as a discussant. Each presenter should prepare a paper on attachment-related pathology surrounding divorce from the expertise viewpoint of the presenter. A general overview of the pathology as described in Article 1 of this petition can be offered to the presenters and discussants to help organize the papers of the invited presenters and the subsequent discussion. The multi-day conference would involve presentation of the papers and general discussion from the participants, resulting in a combined white paper discussing the issues raised, with each individual paper presented in appendices.

This high-level conference of experts could potentially serve as a precursor sub-conference to a larger scale professional conference of experts on the role of professional psychology in its interface with the family court system and child custody decisions. This larger scale conference on the interface of professional psychology in family law child custody decision-making would likely include additional expert participants in parenting and child development factors, assessment methodology, family law representation, and forensic psychology. A precursor high-level conference specifically addressing attachment-related pathology surrounding divorce could help carve out the issues surrounding the assessment, diagnosis, and treatment of attachment-related pathology following divorce as a contributing factor for the subsequent larger scale conference regarding the interface of professional psychology with the legal system in child custody decision-making.

Article 5: Petition Advocacy

Pursuant to Articles 1-3 of this petition, the undersigned urge in the strongest manner possible that the American Psychological Association adopt the remedies described in Article 4.

The lives of children and families are being irrevocably destroyed by the failure of professional psychology to accurately recognize and effectively treat the causes of severe attachment-related family pathology surrounding divorce.

Children have the fundamental right of childhood to love both parents, and to receive the love of both parents in return. We, the undersigned, urge in the strongest manner possible the American Psychological Association to affirm its commitment to achieving professional competence, and ultimately professional expertise, in the assessment, diagnosis, and treatment of children and families as guaranteed in the Ethical Principles of Psychologists and Code of Conduct of the American Psychological Association.

References

Ainsworth, M.D.S. (1989). Attachments beyond infancy. American Psychologist, 44, 709-716.

Bailey, J.M. and Shriver, A. (1999). Does childhood sexual abuse cause borderline personality disorder? Journal of Sex & Marital Therapy, 25, 45-57

Barber, B. K. (Ed.) (2002). Intrusive parenting: How psychological control affects children and adolescents. Washington, DC: American Psychological Association.

Barber, B. K. and Harmon, E. L. (2002). Violating the self: Parenting psychological control of children and adolescents. In B. K. Barber (Ed.), Intrusive parenting (pp. 15-52). Washington, DC: American Psychological Association.

Beck, A.T., Freeman, A., Davis, D.D., & Associates (2004). Cognitive therapy of personality disorders. (2nd edition). New York: Guilford.

Bowen, M. (1978). Family Therapy in Clinical Practice. New York: Jason Aronson.

Bowlby, J. (1969). Attachment and loss. Vol. 1. Attachment, NY: Basic Books.

Bowlby, J. (1973). Attachment and loss: Vol. 2. Separation: Anxiety and anger. NY: Basic.

Bowlby, J. (1980). Attachment and loss: Vol. 3. Loss: Sadness and depression. NY: Basic. Bowlby, J. (1988). A secure base: Parent–child attachment and healthy human development. New York: Basic Books.

Bretherton, I. (1992). The origins of attachment theory: John Bowlby and Mary Ainsworth. Developmental Psychology, 1992, 28, 759-775.

Briand-Malenfant, R., Lecours, S., and Deschenaux, E. (2012). What does sadness mean to BPD patients? Journal of Personality Disorders, 26, 939-955.

Brüne, M., Walden, S., Marc-Andreas, E., Dimaggio, G. (2016). Mentalization of complex emotions in borderline personality disorder: The impact of parenting and exposure to trauma on the performance in a novel cartoon-based task. Comprehensive Psychiatry, 64, 29-37.

Freud, S., & Jones, K. (1939). Moses and monotheism. London: The Hogarth Press and the Institute of psycho-analysis.

Goldenberg H, Goldenberg I. (2013). Family therapy: An overview. 8th ed. Florence, KY: Brooks/Cole Publishing/Cengage Learning

Haley, J. (1977). Toward a theory of pathological systems. In P. Watzlawick & J. Weakland (Eds.), The interactional view (pp. 31-48). New York: Norton.

Kerig, P.K. (2005). Revisiting the construct of boundary dissolution: A multidimensional perspective. Journal of Emotional Abuse, 5, 5-42.

Kernberg, O.F. (1975). Borderline conditions and pathological narcissism. New York: Aronson.

Levy, K.N. (2005). The implications of attachment theory and research for understanding borderline personality disorder. Development and Psychopathology, 17, p. 959-986

Linehan, M. M. & Koerner, K. (1993). Behavioral theory of borderline personality disorder. In J. Paris (Ed.), *Borderline Personality Disorder: Etiology and Treatment*. Washington, D.C.: American Psychiatric Press, 103-21.

Minuchin, S. (1974). Families and Family Therapy. Harvard University Press.

Minuchin. S. & Nichols, M.P. (1993). Family healing: Strategies for hope and understanding. New York: Touchstone.

Ogata, S. N., Silk, K. R., Goodrich, S., Lohr, N. E., Westen, D., & Hill, E. M. (1990). Childhood sexual and physical abuse in adult patients with borderline personality disorder. *The American Journal of Psychiatry, 147*(8), 1008-13.

Raineki, C., Moriceau, S., Sullivan, R.M. (2010). Developing a neurobehavioral animal model of infant attachment to an abusive caregiver. Biological Psychiatry, 67, 1137-1145.

Seay, B. Alexander, B.K., and Harlow, H.F. (1964). Maternal behavior of socially deprived rhesus monkeys. Journal of Abnormal and Social Psychology, 69, 345-354

Sieswerda, S., Arntz, A., Mertens, I., and Vertommen, S. (2006). Hypervigilance in patients with borderline personality disorder: Specificity, automaticity, and predictors. Behavior Research and Therapy, 45, 1011-1024

Soenens, B., & Vansteenkiste, M. (2010). A theoretical upgrade of the concept of parental psychological control: Proposing new insights on the basis of self-determination theory. Developmental Review, 30, 74–99.

Stepp, S. D., Whalen, D. J., Pilkonis, P. A., Hipwell, A. E., & Levine, M. D. (2011). Children of mothers with Borderline Personality Disorder: Identifying parenting behaviors as potential targets for intervention. Personality Disorders: Theory, Research, and Treatment. 1-16. Advance online publication.

Stone, G., Buehler, C., & Barber, B. K.. (2002) Interparental conflict, parental psychological control, and youth problem behaviors. In B. K. Barber (Ed.), Intrusive parenting: How psychological control affects children and adolescents. Washington, DC.: American Psychological Association.

Titelman, P. (2003). Emotional cutoff in Bowen family systems theory: An Overview. In Emotional cutoff: Bowen family systems theory perspectives, P. Tetelman (ed). New York: Haworth Press.

Trippany, R.L., Helm, H.M. and Simpson, L. (2006). Trauma reenactment: Rethinking borderline personality disorder when diagnosing sexual abuse survivors. Journal of Mental Health Counseling, 28, 95-110.

van der Kolk, B.A. (1987). The separation cry and the trauma response: Developmental issues in the psychobiology of attachment and separation. In B.A. van der Kolk (Ed.) Psychological Trauma (31-62). Washington, D.C.: American Psychiatric Press, Inc.

van der Kolk, B.A. (1987). The psychological consequences of overwhelming life experiences. In B.A. van der Kolk (Ed.) Psychological Trauma (1-30). Washington, D.C.: American Psychiatric Press, Inc.

van der Kolk, B.A. (1989). The compulsion to repeat the trauma: Re-enactment, revictimization, and masochism. Psychiatric Clinics of North America, 12, 389-411.